FISHING

THE TOTAL FISHING GUIDE FOR A NOVICE:
SALTWATER TO FRESHWATER

By

Mathew Orton

FREE BONUS: "Click The Link Below To Receive Your Bonus

https://publishfs.leadpages.co/pangea-health/

INTRODUCTION

Ah, fishing! The word conjures up sensations that are at once peaceful and victorious. There is nothing like pitting your skills against nature in an element not your own – water – and coming out the winner. However, for those of you who have just started out or are thinking of starting out, fishing can be an intimidating pursuit. There is so much jargon associated with it and listening to the experts can only serve to confuse you.

In this book, I've tried to make the art of fishing a simple endeavor for the novice. Here you will find all you need to know about the different types of fishing, how to select your gear, what a rig is and what are the different types of rigs, how to set them up and much more! I've also tried to give you a bit of background on fishing and how it started out at first. I've also given you an overview on how to go about fishing in different bodies of water from your basic pond to the vast oceans.

I hope that you find the information in this book useful and helpful in your endeavor to become a skilled fisherman. Consider this a starting point in your journey to becoming the talk o' the tavern and think of all the stories you'll have to tell. Happy Fishing!

CONTENTS

CHAPTER 1

HISTORY OF FISHING

Fishing is an old practice that goes back to the start of the Upper Paleolithic period around 40,000 years ago. Isotopic investigation of the skeletal remnants of Tianyuan man, a 40,000-year-old eastern Asian modern human, has demonstrated that he consistently ate freshwater fish. Archeology components, for example, shell scraps, remains of fish bones, and paintings in caves demonstrate that sea foods were critical for survival and eaten in large amounts.

Throughout this period, the vast majority carried on with a hunter-gatherer way of life and, as such, moved around a lot. Nevertheless, where there are early cases of permanent settlements, for example, those at Lepenski Vir, they are quite often connected with fishing as the dominant source of sustenance.

The early development of fishing for recreational purposes is uncertain. For instance, there is narrative proof for fly fishing in Japan. Nonetheless, fly fishing was probably a way of survival, as opposed to amusement. One of the earliest English articles on recreational fishing was printed in 1496, by Dame Juliana Berners, who was the prioress of the Benedictine Sopwell Nunnery. The exposition was titled Treatyse of Fysshynge wyth an Angle, and included point by point data on waters meant for fishing, the development of lines and rods, and the utilization of natural baits and manufactured flies.

Recreational angling took an incredible jump forward after the English Civil War, where a newfound enthusiasm for the action left an impression on the numerous books and treatises that were composed on the subject at the time. In 1653, Izaak Walton wrote the Compleat Angler which depicted the fishing in the Derbyshire Wye. It was a tribute to the workmanship and soul of fishing in writing and verse. A second part to the book was written by Walton's companion Charles Cotton.

Charles Kirby invented an enhanced fishing hook in 1655 that has not been modified much till now. He also invented the Kirby twist later, a special hook with a counterbalance point that is used to this day.

The eighteenth century was basically a time of combination of the techniques that had evolved in the earlier century. Running rings started to show up along the fishing rods, which gave fishermen more noteworthy control over the cast line. Depending upon which type of fishing one was interested in, the rods were also designed to be more refined and elaborate. By the time the middle of the century rolled around, one could see jointed rods almost everywhere. Also, to make the rod more flexible and stronger, manufacturers used bamboo for the top portion of the rod.

The sport had also become quite commercial – one could find tackle and rods for sale at the haberdasher's store. The Great Fire of London forced artisans to move to Redditch. Redditch then became the production hub for fishing related items in the early 18th century. Onesimus Ustonson built up his shop in 1761, which became the leader in the market for another 100 years. This leadership was recognised by the monarch in the form of a Royal Warrant that was granted to him and he then became the official provider of tackle to three consecutive rulers beginning with King George IV over this period. He additionally created the multiplying winch. The commercialization of the business came during a period of extended enthusiasm for fishing as a recreational side interest for individuals from the aristocracy.

The influence of the Industrial Revolution could be first seen in how the fly lines were manufactured. Earlier fishing enthusiasts had to twist their own lines - an arduous and tedious process. The new spinning machines that spun textile made it easy for tapered lines to be produced and sold.

English fly-fishing kept on evolving in the nineteenth Century, with the rise of fly fishing clubs, alongside the publication of quite a few books on the subject of fly tying and fly fishing strategies.

By the mid to late nineteenth century, growing recreational opportunities lower and middle classes started to have an impact on fly fishing, which had a growing appeal to the masses and not just the aristocracy. The extension of the railroad in Britain permitted the less well-off to take weekend treks to the ocean side or to streams for angling. Wealthier specialists went abroad. The substantial waterways of Norway loaded with extensive supplies of salmon started to draw in fishing enthusiasts from England in hordes by the middle of the century - Jones' Guide to Norway, and Salmon-Fisher's Pocket Partner, distributed in 1848, was composed by Frederic Tolfrey and was a well-known guidebook for the country.

CHAPTER 2

BEGINNER'S GUIDE TO FISHING

GEAR UP

All sports pull in their share of gear obsessed freaks. At the same time, it's difficult to envision one that confuses the novice with a more extensive scope of contrivances and doohickeys than does fishing. You can purchase a different reel and rod combo for pretty much any type of water that you're ever going to fish in, manufactured baits for any conceivable mix of water conditions and quarry and everything else from electric hook sharpeners to self-warming streamside seats. Also, as your quest for fish brings you down varying trails, a great deal of those things may well become absolute necessities. For the time being, however, I'm going to attempt to set you up with an adaptable, do-most-anything apparatus, which won't mess up your budget for food.

The heart of your outfit, obviously, will be the reel and rod. Also, since we're attempting to choose a basic, flexible, pretty much idiot-proof rig, your best choices are 1) a spin-casting set, 2) a bait-casting outfit or 3) an open-faced spinning reel and the rod to match. There are eager fanatics of every choice, and any variety will work out, yet I'm going to recommend that you buy an open-face reel of medium size (one appropriate for line in the six to 10-pound test range; ask the sales representative to load it with as much as it will hold when you get it) and a six-to seven-foot fiberglass, medium action spinning rod. (You should see the action on a label on the rod.) With this apparatus, some lures and some sinkers and hooks, which will be mentioned below, you ought to be able to fish for most freshwater fish, in many types of water, and even catch the smaller saltwater species.

While many people may suggest a spin-casting, or closed-faced, reel for the novice, I favor the open-faced on the grounds that it's easy to work and, well, open. At the point when the line tangles in the middle of a cast (trust me, it will), you will be able to untangle that mess without dismantling the reel itself. Also, although an open-faced spinning rig may take somewhat more practice than the closed faced version, I think it offers much more control and casting distance.

Obviously, you will need to practice as much as possible. Luckily, all you have to finish your preparation are an open field or expansive back yard and a little (1/4-to 1/2-ounce) lead sinker. Simply attach the weight to the end of your line and keep in mind the directions in the sidebar. Try not to be disheartened when your first tries at casting fizzle out. The right touch and rhythm will come rapidly, and in a brief while your precision and casting range to permit you to keep on improving your abilities while you're fishing!

TERMINAL TACKLE

Despite the fact that the term sounds scary, terminal handle just means the sinkers, hooks, bobbers and artificial baits that you'll be securing to the end of your line before you cast for fish. Again, you have an overwhelming number of choices. However, some fundamental purchases ought to set you up to start.

A BIT ABOUT BAIT

The good thing about artificial lures is that you can catch fish with them and they don't stink when left for too long in the fridge. Yet live bait can't be beat. For freshwater fishing, you won't find a better bait than the earthworm (it isn't called angleworm just because). Other great options are minnows (ensure the ones you utilize are local to the water you're fishing in . . . "imports" may get you the fish, but can also disrupt the ecological balance if a few escape). Crawfish (also known as crawdads) are useful, as well, especially in the spring and early summer, when they've shed one exoskeleton and not yet grown another completely. ("Softshells" are one of the unequaled traps for smallmouth bass.) Other options for fresh water can be crickets, frogs, different lizards, grasshoppers, hellgrammites and whatever else fish routinely eat.

A wide variety of saltwater lures are, likewise, available. In the event that you choose to do sea angling, make a few inquiries at your neighborhood trap shop or dock and learn what works best and what doesn't. (Cut mullet, bloodworms, sandworms, shrimp and squid are some top choices.)

WETTING THE LINE

The fishing strategies you'll utilize will depend on the water you're fishing in and the species you would like to catch. Simply pick the one that is nearest to the setting in which you'll be angling, and the advice I dispense ought to give you a reliable point from which to begin. Be that as it may, don't let anybody's recommendation keep you from observing and learning from the veterans around you. Each pond, stream, lake and waterway has its own peculiarities. You could fish in one range for a lifetime and not know all the secrets it has so you're surely not going to get all that you have to know here.

THE FARM POND

It's difficult to envision a more pleasant setting for "jist sittin' an' fishin'." The air will most likely convey the fragrance of worked soil and wildflowers (and some cow). Swallows will fly overhead, and the surface of the water may swell once in a while with the interesting lump of a surfacing turtle. Even better, there can be a wealth of fish in farm ponds. You'll normally see bream, catfish of some sort, largemouth bass and such "waste" fish as carp or suckers. On the off chance that the pond is sufficiently deep and remains chilly and oxygen-rich year-round, it might even be loaded with trout. (It's a given that you would do well to get approval before fishing in someone else's pond. A well-kept, supplied pond speaks to a major interest in time, cash and work, and the trespasser is as liable to get a heap of birdshot as a string of bream.)

The most widely recognized approach to fish a farm pond, or some other little, still waterway, is with a hook, bobber, worms (either red worms or night crawlers) and a little split shot sinker. Remember that, "You can get a big fish on a small hook easier than you can get a small fish on a large one." I propose beginning with a number six or eight. Just string the worm on the hook—leave enough hanging free to get a tempting squirm, but make sure to cover the point of the hook—clasp the split-shot a couple inches to a foot or so over the lure, alter the bobber to the line at a point where it will glide the worm simply over the base or over any submerged foliage and flip the whole thing into a spot that looks likely. It's a good idea to fish near an area where there is some type of cover: lily pads, a dock, and so forth.

Make sure that the line is tight but not so tight that the bobber drags along. An intrigued fish will presumably first show itself by "nibbling," making the float tremble, snap forward and backward, or move up and down. That is your signal to focus. However, don't do anything yet. At the point when the fish drags the bobber along the surface of the water with assurance or pulls it under, give a short, sharp twitch of the bar to set the hook, and reel in your prize.

In the event that you plan to return the fish to the water, wet your hands before touching it, and handle it tenderly. (In case you've decided to release your day's catch, it's best to use a pair of pliers to twist down the barbs or points on your hooks, to remove the hook easily.) Whether you mean to release the fish or not, take a few moments to enjoy its delicacy of shading and magnificence of line. Not many things look as alive as a living fish, and valuing that magnificence is one of your prizes for skillful fishing. Appreciate it.

At that point, once you've unfastened the fish and put it on a stringer or in a water-filled bucket, rebait your hook and cast back in to the same spot. Odds are you will find more where the first one came from.

However, if a while goes by with your bobber doing nothing more than serving as a landing place for tired dragonflies, reel it in, examine the bait to ensure you weren't napping or diverted when a fish bit and attempt another area on the lake. You can also vary the depth of the bait you're using by moving the bobber up and down. You may even make a generally long cast and move the float a foot or so consistently or two until you discover fish. In a reasonably stocked pond, a couple of hours of this kind of rest and unwinding should give you the makings of a decent family supper.

There are, obviously, less restful approaches to handle the same pond. What's more, although bobber angling can yield some enormous fish, the strategies mentioned above are much more likely to bring you bream than big trout or bass.

In case largemouth bass are what you're after, you'll most likely do well with a variety of the bobber strategy. Simply attempt a greater float and a greater hook (measure two or bigger) and a two-inch long (or more) shiner or minnow, hooked either through the lips or simply under the back (dorsal) balance so it can swim uninhibitedly. The little baitfish will pull the bobber around, yet you shouldn't experience any difficulty recognizing the difference in the way the float moves when a bass gets the trap and tries to snatch it.

With that "hawg" (bass-fishing' talk for a really large one) as a main priority, this is most likely a decent time to discuss drag. Either on top of your reel's spool or by the handle (see the proprietor's manual) will be a dial you can extricate or fix to make it simpler or harder to draw line off the closed spool. Set this to permit the line to be taken when the draw turns out to be more than half of the breaking strength of the line (you can guesstimate precisely enough). At that point, when a genuine hawg takes off on a run, he'll basically pull against the drag, tiring himself at the same time, rather than breaking free. Try to keep the tip of the rod high, once he is on the hook and fighting. Also try to reel the line in only when the hawg isn't pulling. On the off chance that the bass detonates upward in a rainbow-showering jump, drop the rod tip a foot or so every time the fish breaks water. Attempt to make your maneuvers smooth, progressive yet tenacious. With a little good fortune, you'll soon get the bass' lower lip (watch that hook) and heave your prize on to the shore.

You can likewise fish for pond bass (or trout) with any of the draws I suggested. Simply cast the spoons and weighted spinners toward a reasonable looking spot and reel in. Keep changing how deep you go to retrieve fish by giving the bait a chance to sink to varying depths before you start to reel the line in. Attempt different types of retrieves - quick, moderate and jerky. Once more, give careful consideration to conceivable cover, and fish as near it as you can. You'll lose a couple baits to obstacles along these lines, at the same time, "In case you aren't getting hung up, you likely aren't catching anything."

There are numerous approaches to fish plastic worms (truth be told, there are entire books on the subject). One of the simplest and best is to fix the worm with a huge hook and egg or bullet sinker, cast it out and skip it over the base by raising and bringing down the rod tip while reeling gradually. Attempt to build up a vibe for what the worm is doing. A strike may not be dramatic or immediately visible. More often than not, a bass will basically take a worm in its mouth as the hook is dropping (when you bring down your rod tip) and hold it. At whatever point the lure appears to stop in a manner that is not natural, react by lifting the rod tip firmly so that the hook is set.

The Jitterbug is a surface bait, and presumably best at sunset, or even at night. Cast the jitterbug near areas which have cover, let it sit till the swells created by its sprinkling down vanish and attempt distinctive rates of retrieval. It's regularly successful just to "pop" the 'bug in with short jolts of the rod, giving the bug a chance to rest after every bounce. A striking fish will more often than not hook itself. Simply raise the rod tip when you feel the hit, and battle the lunker to shore.

LAKES, SLOW RIVERS AND OCEAN SHORES

Any strategies that work in a homestead pond will work in bigger waterways—if the artificial lures are meant for the fish that are accessible or in the event that you utilize fitting bait. When it comes to large water bodies, though, another type of still-fishing is known to be quite effective. Known as bottom fishing, it requires a heavier sinker and at least one hooks to hold the lure on, or a little above, the bottom after a (typically) long cast.

Bottom fishing normally calls for live bait and one of the terminal rigs. Watch what other fisher folk, particularly the effective ones, are utilizing. When all is said in done, it's best to keep a tight line so you can see the sharp rapping on the rod tip that flags an encouraging fish, or feel that electric snapping on a fingertip. (To do this, squeeze the line, simply over the reel, between your thumb and pointer.)

In the event that you have admittance to a pontoon, you can cover a considerable measure of water by trolling a man-made lure behind the moving boat. Coordinate the pontoon's speed to the "activity" (wobble, spin or flash) of your lure (for the most part an open to paddling speed or moderate speed should work). Release some line and sit tight for the activity. When you have a strike, you can grapple in the spot and cast draws, or attempt live lure, or troll forward and backward over the territory a couple of more times to check whether your first catch was a piece of a school.

STREAMS AND FAST RIVERS

A wide range of fish possess large amounts of streams and quickly moving waterways, however when this sort of water rings a bell, we think trout. Furthermore, to be honest, when trout ring a bell, most fishermen think fly-angling, a great and sly game that is past the extent of this essential article. Ought to your angling yen move in this course, there are any number of fine books on the subject. You can, in any case, explore different avenues regarding dry (coasting) and wet (sinking) flies with your turning outfit. To do as such, simply purchase a "throwing bubble," which is a reasonable bobber that gives the mass important to flip an almost weightless fly on turning tackle, then fish the water as you would with live lure, a method that is inside the extent of this piece.

At the point when trout are the quarry, the worm is the most normally utilized live draw. Truth be told, a considerable number of trout are discovered by as yet angling—either on the base or with a bobber, in the profound, moderate moving pools of streams and waterways. Night crawlers are the regular as yet angling trap, yet—for my cash—a sound garden dug red worm will outflank a crawler in as yet angling, and is very nearly an unquestionable requirement on the off chance that you need to "work" a stream like a fly-angler.

For this method, a demonstrated fish catcher and in addition a brilliant reason to investigate the tumbling, shade-and daylight dappled staircases of a mountain stream, you'll require your littlest hooks, a couple of small split-shot sinkers and a leader. Just a length of line of various quality from what's on the reel's

spool, a leader—for our motivations here—comprises of a four-
to six-foot area of two-to four-pound test line that will be less
obvious to trout in gin-clear water than the "working" line on
the reel. Tie this leader on, then, with the little hook and a worm
set up (hook the worm just through the head, so the vast
majority of its length dangles openly), try different things with
various weights of split shot by dropping the worm, with the
weight settled six creeps above it, into the current before you.
Your point is to pick a weight that will permit the worm to sink
against the current at around a 45-degree edge, then let it move
along the base normally.

Once your apparatus is right, continue upstream, strolling in the
water (pants and tennis shoes ought to suffice in everything
except the coldest streams), flipping the trap in front of you,
more often than not at an edge toward the bank, in a manner
that it will float underneath undercut banks, into the whirlpool
washes framed by rocks, under tree appendages anticipating
into the stream and—by and large—wherever the blend of ebb
and flow provided sustenance and slower-than-ordinary water

shows a sensible resting place for a ravenous trout. This will all take practice, obviously. Remember that the water around you is clear, and that trout are eccentric. Move gradually. Hold up a moment or more in the wake of getting into position before flipping your lure to a promising spot, and—as when angling lakes with plastic worms—consider any unnatural faltering in the float of your hook to be a striking fish.

On waters, sufficiently huge to permit longer throwing, your weighted spinners can likewise be viable. Once more, work from a position in the stream itself, either throwing upstream, past promising concealing spots, then reeling sufficiently quick to advance the bait of the flow, or downstream, throwing toward the bank at an edge so the moving water clears the draw out toward midstream as you reel. In either case, recollect where strikes happen, and be perceptive. The way to stream angling is building up a feeling of what's happening under the water by watching its surface.

CHAPTER 3

DIFFERENT TYPES OF FISHING

FRESHWATER FISHING

There are freshwater lakes, supplies, lakes, streams and waterways in each state the nation over that are incorporated into the rundown of the best places to angle. Freshwater angling is one of the sorts of angling that is perfect for starting fishermen since it can be delighted in from shore or from land utilizing a basic handle set up. There are numerous sorts of freshwater fish, for example, largemouth bass or bluegill, which can be focused by the whole family with an essential bar and reel combo.

It has been estimated that freshwater species make up about 40 percent of all fish. Regular freshwater fish species are certain salmon, trout, bass, musky, walleye, crappie and quite a few others.

Freshwater angling should be possible from multiple points of view – from shore or a vessel, from a scaffold or dock, in lakes and lakes, and waterways and streams. There is an assortment of freshwater angling methods, notwithstanding gear, hooks and baits, contingent upon the kind of fish you're after.

With all the diverse potential outcomes, there's something for everybody. What are you sitting tight for?

SALTWATER FISHING

Novices can target species, for example, spotted seatrout and redfish from shore or from a shallow water pads pontoon, while experienced big game fishermen may like to invest energy saltwater remote ocean looking for seaward species like marlin or fish from an expansive sport fishing watercraft. The sort of angling supplies handle and rigging that is utilized for saltwater angling varies impressively in view of the species and the particular angling systems that are connected.

Saltwater angling is as much about the experience as it is about the fish. A large number of the game fish species can be huge and mean, and the water can be huge and awful. From shallow saltwater pads to profound sea angling, saltwater fishermen pursue everything from dainty spotted trout to gigantic blue marlin in probably the most exceptional and helpful surroundings on earth.

Saltwater angling can be as straightforward or as mind boggling as you wish. Tenderfoots can begin angling from the shoreline with essential handle and a modest bunch of saltwater apparatuses Then keep on honing your aptitudes and attempt more propelled saltwater angling with the assistance of our saltwater angling tips and traps. Before long you could be an enthusiastic fisher who invests interminable energy seaward getting prized sportfish.

Whether you live along the 10,000 miles of U.S. coastline or are going to the sea for the weekend, there are a lot of chances to wet a line. And, of course, you will find plenty of fish in the sea.

ICE FISHING

Ice angling gives fishermen a chance to go angling amid the colder months of the year. A one of a kind affair, ice angling can offer fishermen an opportunity to angle any spot of a lake or stream without a watercraft. It can likewise offer people an opportunity to get outside, take in the winter air and appreciate time with family and companions.

Ice angling is packed in specific regions of the nation where the climate licenses ice to thicken enough to walk, however that does not mean the movement is constrained to the individuals who live in those territories. It requires diverse instruments and strategies than new or salt water angling. When you have been on the ice and attempted the game, you may discover you like ice angling the same amount of, perhaps more, than different sorts of angling.

This kind of angling includes the utilization of an ice wood screw to penetrate gaps into the ice on a solidified lake, lake or waterway and after that getting fish on hooks and lines through the openings in the ice. To give security from the wind and cool, fishermen regularly angle within ice shanties or compact sanctuaries.

FLY FISHING

To begin fly angling you require a fly bar, a line and some simulated flies. The thought is to catch angle by inspiring them to nibble on an impersonation of a bug or goad angle on, or just underneath, the water. Flies are made utilizing string, wire, dots, quills, yarn and hair, and are made to look like bugs and draw angle at different phases of development to pull in trout, salmon, container fish and carp, and also marine species, for example, tarpon, bone fish and striped bass.

The vast majority consider fly angling as a game best delighted in mountain streams with gets of trout and salmon. In spite of the fact that these sorts of waters are incredible spots to fly fish, you can likewise appreciate astonishing fly angling in the warm waters of lakes and lakes, and in salt water - and get an expansive exhibit of fish. There's presumably a waterway you can use for fly angling not very a long way from where you live.

Fly angling includes the utilization of simulated flies to catch angle in either crisp or saltwater. The fly is thrown into the water utilizing particular rigging, which incorporates a fly pole, reel, and weighted line. This strategy for angling utilizes systems that are more testing than different sorts of angling since it includes throwing a light-weight fly rather than a heavier draw or characteristic lure. Fly angling methods and apparatus will fluctuate contingent upon the living space.

POLE FISHING

Pole fishing is a very particular variant of float fishing. Poles give a level of accuracy that a rod and reel can't deliver.

Why is pole fishing one of the best methods for freshwater fishing?

One of the first reasons for its efficacy is bait presentation. The fishing enthusiast has steady control over the rig because the distance between the float and the tip of the pole is so short. To make the hook bait appeal to any fish there are a variety of techniques you can use – you can hold the float still, you can slow it down in a current, you can move it left to right at different speeds, or even just lift it up and down. Sometimes all you have to do is just duplicate the moves that nature makes. You just need to try to match how the natural forage lays or moves at the bottom. You can also use bait that resembles insects in the area or other small prey that live in those waters.

Accuracy is another reason that pole fishing really works. Since we use ground bait to draw fish under the pole tip, the hook doesn't move far and wide. Instead it is fixed in a small and concentrated area of feed and therefore, just in front of the mouth of the fish!

The third advantage is that you can fish with the lightest of tackle (this means that you can use a float that is smaller in size, a smaller-sized hook and a more slender line). After all, since the lighter tackle is not as easily visible to the fish, it ends up producing more bites.

Poles can be utilized to fish in all sorts of freshwater bodies – from fast or shallow rivers to farm ponds to really large lakes. You can buy poles of varying designs, lengths and strengths. You can use them to catch many different types of fish ranging from the tiny roach to salmon or even carp. As mentioned above, with poles you can fish with a much greater level of efficacy and accuracy. Not only is pole fishing popular with match fishermen, but it is also used to great effect by professionals. The results can be seen in the large amounts of fish that are caught. Poles are designed to be long, big and tapering. They end in a fine tip. You need to tie the line of the float rig to the end of the pole tip. You can also attach a piece of elastic to the pole tip or inside the tip and then attach the float rig to the end of the elastic. The elastic will help you when you need to fight fish. The float rig you attach is suspended from the tip of the pole and is pushed into the water. You can vary the length of the line between the pole tip and the float depending upon what type of fishing you are indulging in and where.

There are some methods that can be utilized to land fish on a pole.

• Dallying – You can dabble the bait next to tight spots such as riverbanks, stumps and holes in the moss beds.

- Sling-shot – You can use this method when you have to get your lure under structures such as docks or branches. You'll need to hold the hook by the bend and pull back so that there is tension on the pole and then release.

- Walking – You can troll along a riverbank that doesn't have any obstructions.

- Tire the fish – This is one of the most well-known techniques. All you have to do is make the fish swim around until it is completely tuckered out and then reel it in.

- Tricking – You can use this method when you want to trick the bigger fish into swimming into your landing net. Once the fish is hooked, push the pole tip away from you and past the fish. This way the fish is between you and the pole. Then put a bit of pressure on the line. This will make the fish swim away from the pressure and straight into your landing net.

BAIT CASTING

This style of fishing uses a heavy lure that pulls the line into the target area. You use a free spool or revolving-spool reel that has been attached to the rod on the top side. Bait casting is not easy and is definitely something that requires knowhow and practice. Once you're used to the method, you will be able to cast your bait accurately into spots where the fish feed and can generally be found. Since the whole technique is dependent upon the weight of the lure, you need larger bait. You can cast them for a longer distance.

SPIN CASTING

Spin casting is a perfect angling technique for novice fishermen. Professionals also use it to fish for bass. The technique is much easier than bait casting and can be used with both heavy and light lures with no worries about tangling up the line or breaking it. For spin casting, you can use a spin-cast reel, a closed-face reel or an open-face reel.

DOBU OR KOROGASHI FISHING

This is an old-school Japanese fly fishing method, which has been in use since the times of the feudal lords. The rig involved is a sinker rig which uses a group of wet flies. This method was popular as a sport in western Japan, especially around Kyoto, where craftsmen had perfected the art of working the fly-patterns. This uses a long rod that ranges from nine to eleven meters and a four to five meter leader that has around three to four droppers and a tenbin boom with a sinker on one end and an additional dropper at the other end. You extend the rig into the water, lower it to the depth you want, and then move it around until it reaches the most downstream part of the water. This is usually used to catch dace, chub and ayu.

TENKARA FISHING

Tenkara is another traditional Japanese fly fishing technique. It uses one soft hackle fly to catch mountain creek trout such as iwana and yamame. Even today, tenkara is most popular among fresh-water fishermen in Japan who are interested in fishing for small stream trout. It is most effective when fishing in faster streams or pocket water. Some advantages it has over other methods are being able to hold the line off the water, greater control over the fly, precision casting, light line with delicate presentations and an elegant simplicity to the whole method.

The traditional materials used for tenkara are a rod made of bamboo, a taper line made of horse tail and a tippet made of silk. The fly patterns are soft hackle that mostly covers beneath the film on the surface. Modern tenkara materials include high grade carbon fiber or fiberglass rods that are strong and light and a 5:5 reflex for a level line and 3:7 reflex for a taper line. The lines are made from fluorocarbon and western dry fly patterns are fairly common. The handles are made of cork or wood. The line is what moves the weightless fly ahead. Common rigs generally use a running line (level or tapered) that is between four to seven meters. A four pound test leader that is between thirty centimeters and one meter is tied to the end of the line. The size of the stream determines the length of the running line. The leader is tied to the tip of the rod so that dapping can be done in the deepest parts of the stream. Furled lines have the advantages of being easy to cast and having a delicate presentation that make them easier to cast against the wind. The fly is connected to the line using a regular fly-fishing tippet because the line is too thick to be tied directly to the fly. Tenkara fly-fishing uses artificial flies that are tied with fur, feathers or thread – the way they are tied in western fly-fishing. The traditional fly is known as 'kebari' and is a special reverse-hackle wet fly.

AYU FISHING

Ayu fishing is one of the specialized styles of fly-fishing in Japan that originated more than four hundred years ago. It came into being when fishermen discovered that dressing the fly with pieces of cloth could fool the fish into biting. The samurai, who were not allowed to practice sword fighting or any type of martial art during the Edo era, discovered that this style was a good alternative for regular training. The rod became a substitute for the sword and walking and balancing on the small stones in streams helped train their balance and legs. Since only the samurai were allowed to fish, they made their own hooks by bending sewing needles and also fashioned their flies by hand.

This style of fishing needs rods that are five to seven meters in length and, of course, flies. However, you don't need fly-casting. You can even use decoy fish instead of flies. Because ayu fish can be quite territorial, they attack the decoy fish.

DAPPING

While dapping is considered a style of fly-fishing, you shouldn't confuse tenkara fly-fishing with dapping. Dapping covers a range of techniques from the ancient to the modern. You can just move the fly up and down on the water or you can use the blow line that allows the wind to carry the fly to the fish. Dapping can use both a tenkara fly-fishing rod and a modern rod. A short rod, however, won't be quite as efficacious.

The rods used for dapping can be as long as forty feet and the dappers used today can also use reels. These reels need to allow for a quick retrieval and shouldn't let the blow line get wet. In dapping, you just need to let the wind do the work; it blows the line out and then drops the fly where it needs to go while moving it around enough to make it seem lifelike.

STILL FISHING

Sometimes the easiest fishing technique can also be the best. As the name implies, still-fishing means that you simply put your lure in the water and wait for a fish to bite. How far below the surface your lure should go depends upon what you want to catch and how deep the water itself is. You can fish on the bottom, lower your bait to somewhere in the middle or just fish near the surface of the water. If you want to fish near the surface, use a bobber or a float. If, however, you want the bait to go deeper, use sinkers on your line.

You can still-fish in a number of ways – sitting on a dock, boat or bridge in rivers, ponds, streams and lakes at any time of the day. The thing to remember here is that you need to be very patient. The fish will bite but in their own time.

DRIFT FISHING

As the name suggest, drift fishing is done when your boat is drifting, not anchored. Because your boat is drifting around you have the advantage of being able to fish over a variety of different fishing grounds depending upon the wind and the currents. You can change the depth you're fishing at by attaching floats or bobbers if you want to fish near the surface or attaching sinkers to the line if you want to fish near or on the bottom. In this style of fishing it is best to use natural or live bait. You can also use artificial flies, lures and jigs. Drift fishing can be done on ponds, lakes, streams and rivers at any time of the year.

LIVE LINING

Live lining is done in a flowing rather than still body of water such as streams or rivers. You don't allow the boat to drift; instead, you anchor it to one spot and use prepared or live bait. The bait should either be on the bottom or just off the bottom of the river or stream. When you live line off the bottom, your line moves with the current and goes through rocks and holes in which the fish may be hiding.

CHUMMING

To draw in fish or make them bite once more, you can toss "chum" into the water where you're angling. You can utilize ground-up fish bait, dead minnows in an espresso can (for ice fishing), canned sweet corn, and even pet food or breakfast oat. You can also scrape the bottom using an oar to stir up some natural chum. Make sure that you don't over-chum. You want them intrigued enough to feed, not so stuffed with food that they don't go for your hook. Chumming is not lawful in all states. Check nearby fishing controls.

BASE BOUNCING

Base bouncing is a technique used when you're sitting in a boat that is drifting or is trolling. It is an effective way to attract fish throughout most of the year and during most times of the day. In order to base bounce, you need natural bait or a buck tail jig that you drag along the bottom. The dragging movement makes the lure bounce along the bottom and stirs up mud or sand. Once you've had a few strikes using this method, anchor the boat in one spot and use other techniques to fish for whatever types of fish you're interested in.

TROLLING

Trolling is done by propelling the boat through the water, using a small motor so that the movement isn't enough to scare the fish away. However, a boat isn't always necessary. You can also troll while sitting on bridge or a pier by moving the lure through the water while walking alongside it. The depth of the bait is determined by how fast you move. Of course, you also need to keep in mind the fish you're trying to catch and at what depth they generally swim. It is best to use a bait caster or spinning reel for trolling.

JIGGING

Jig angling is well known and tests your skills. In jigging, it is the person who is fishing and their actions that attract the fish. Here's how to do it. Cast out your jig hook and allow it to sink right to the bottom. Now, raise the jig about a foot off the bottom by using your rod tip and then let it drop down again. You don't just need to do an up and down movement. You can also try right to left or vice versa or even forward and backward. Jigs are available in a variety of sizes and shapes and the best part is that you don't need live bait here.

JIG AND WORM

This technique is a variation of jigging with, of course, a worm attached to the jig. You can use this to either sweep through the waters or bottom hop. To sweep, you'll need to cast out to where you know the fish are, drag the jig in a motion that makes it move parallel to the bottom and do this while you reel in keeping the line taut. If you want to bottom hop, cast out to the target area and allow the jig to sink in. Once the jig is in, start reeling the line in slowly and move the rod very slightly at every third or fourth turn of the reel. Remember, slow and steady gets the fish.

CATCH AND RELEASE

Catch and release was thought up as a means of allowing fishing enthusiasts to indulge while avoiding overfishing and lowering the cost of stocking trout that were hatchery-raised. The method was first used in Michigan. It caught on thanks to both sport fishermen and conservatives because it allows sustainable fishing. There are techniques in place that reduce the need to fight fish and the handling times. These techniques are meant to avoid damage to the fish that could result in fungal infections once the fish is back in the water.

CHAPTER 4

FISHING GEAR

GEAR SELECTION

Fishing supplies, in the same way as other things, can be classified comprehensively into three classes. The least expensive stuff is almost dependably garbage. I don't prescribe purchasing the least expensive pole or reel you can discover as it won't last and not work well. The following class up of apparatus, the mid-level, ought to work fine and dandy. The top end expensive stuff is incredible to use on the off chance that you can bear the cost of it and once you use it you won't be comfortable with the mid-range gear anymore.

RODS

Before selecting an angling rod, you have to decide what sort of fish you want to get with it. When you do that, you have to make sense of how you will fish for them. Rods will have recommended line rating and lure weight ranges on them. When all is said and done you ought to accept that the bar will perform ideally amidst that range. Take note that the line appraisals go out the window in case you will utilize twisted line. When all is said and done, one-piece rods perform much better than rods that can be separated into various pieces, yet the comfort of having the capacity to separate a rod into shorter pieces is frequently exceptionally significant in this time of airlines that charge excess baggage fees.

Some of the things you want to keep in mind while selecting a pole are feel, weight, length, firmness, taper, and guide material. On the off chance that you hold a pole and it simply doesn't "feel right" you most likely shouldn't get it as it is just going to feel more terrible following a day of throwing with it. You need to get the lightest rod that you can use as this will ensure you don't end up tired when throwing throughout the day. Rods made of graphite are by and large the lightest and also the most sensitive in spite of the fact that they will probably snap more easily than fiberglass bars. In the event that you drop them or hit them against something, the graphite can weaken and cause the rod to all of a sudden smash when battling a fish.

Longer rods are useful for distance casts, while shorter rods permit you more leverage when you are reeling in a fish, particularly from a boat. Longer rods can be awkward in the event that you are angling in tight ranges with thick vegetation, so that is something you will want to keep in mind. Consider the spots you will fish in and then make your choice. Are you planning to go bottom fishing from a boat? You might want to get a shorter rod so you can use its leverage. If you're planning to do long distance casts in open water, a longer rod may be your best bet. Seven feet is a decent all-around length.

The stiffness of the rod is critical and changes depending upon what type of fishing you plan to do. In case you plan to fish for bigger fish or will cast lures that are heavy, you will require a stiffer rod. In the event that you are fishing for smaller fish a thin, light, delicate tip may be the distinction between feeling a nibble and not feeling anything. Likewise, it is unpleasant to horse in little fish on stiff rods. Additionally it is harder to cast sensitive live hooks with firm rods; you require a tip which has a little give.

The taper of a rod is likewise critical. "Fast-taper" rods tend to bend close to the tip, while "slow-taper" rods have a parabolic bend that is even. I, by and large, lean toward fast-taper rods for the greater part considering the types of fishing I do. They have a tendency to have more lifting force.

Guide material is imperative too. Less expensive guides have a tendency to be heavier, adding to the general weight of the rod. Likewise, less expensive guide materials may not hold up in case braided line is being used. In the event that your line cuts into the guide it breaks. In the event that you are going to fish with braided line, ensure the guides can take it. Check your guides on a regular basis; on the off chance that they are scratched even a little you'll need to change them since they will mess up your line.

As you get more interested in fishing (or your budget has more give) you might need to investigate custom rods. These can be particularly made to fit you and in addition the sort of fishing you will do. I ought to caution you however, once you go custom it's difficult to do a reversal. Whether you purchase custom or industrial facility wrapped, I truly like the Calstar Grafighter rods for saltwater fishing.

REELS

To me, the reel is the most imperative bit of hardware in case you are focusing on large fish. Specifically, the drag framework on the reel needs to work well if a large fish is pulling hard or your line will snap and end the game. Drag frameworks must be smooth (i.e., apply even weight regardless of the possibility that the fish is pulling in hard starts and stops) and sturdy (i.e. it must not jam up under serious ongoing pressure). I have had various reels jam up on long keeps runs in which big fish are involved, which more often than not ends up with the fish being lost.

There are two primary sorts of reels: Spinning reels and Bait casting or Conventional reels. There are additionally exceptional reels for fly angling however I don't do a lot of that so I'll skirt those.

SPINNING REELS

Spinning reels are phenomenal for novices since they are anything but difficult to utilize. They are anything but difficult to switch between a left gave recover and a privilege gave recover, which is a pleasant element. Throwing is simple - you flip the safeguard over, hold the line with your forefinger, and let go once you snap the pole forward so as to cast. Spinning reels are a fabulous decision for light draws and hooks as a traditional reel will more often than not be hard to cast with weights of 1/8 oz or less. They are not as useful for exactness giving a role as bait casting reels, yet you can even now be exceptionally exact particularly on the off chance that you get the hang of backing the line off with your fingers after you cast.

Spinning reels are seldom utilized for substantial fish (i.e. Marlin trolling) since they don't have a tendency to be as solid as traditional reels and the drag frameworks are not as a rule as great. Likewise, it is harder to produce reel spinning power. In any case, there are some top of the line ones, for example, the Daiwa Saltiga that can deal with some huge fish. I got a 175lb Goliath Grouper on my Daiwa Saltiga Dogfight reel, and in addition a few expansive Giant Trevally.

Actually I truly like the Daiwa Certate spinning reels for freshwater and the Daiwa Dogfight for overwhelming saltwater. These are the main two models of spinning reel that I truly utilize now. They are somewhat top of the line however there are a lot of spinning reels in the mid-level range that function admirably. Most freshwater fish are not going to rip 100 yards off your drag so they don't put as much weight on your handle.

While selecting a spinning reel, I get a kick out of the chance to hold it to feel the weight, and check whether it recovers without much wobble. I additionally get a kick out of the chance to test the counter turn around by reeling advances and after that all of a sudden attempting to reel in reverse. A decent reel ought to stop the turn around reeling quickly; a less expensive reel will give you a chance to reel handle slip back a ¼" or more before ceasing. You need prompt stoppage for good hooksets. A few retailers, for example, Bass Pro Shops likewise have audits.

CONVENTIONAL REELS

Conventional reels have a turning spool that twists when you cast. These by and large have more grounded drag frameworks than turning reels and are less demanding to wrench when there is a considerable measure of weight, however they are harder for tenderfoots to utilize. This is on the grounds that if the spool turns speedier than the line is going out when you cast, you will get a major bunch called a kickback. These can be bad to the point that you in some cases need to cut a lot of line off keeping in mind the end goal to utilize the reel.

The way you maintain a strategic distance from a kickback is to keep some weight on the spool with your thumb as the spool pivots when you cast. This takes some practice and there is somewhat of a craftsmanship to making sense of when to put weight and how much. Most ordinary reels have some kind of throwing control that you can use to back the reel off and decrease kickbacks. Be that as it may, the more you back the spool off the less separation you get. The genuine specialists get a kick out of the chance to utilize zero cast control and do everything with their thumbs. By and by I get a kick out of the chance to have a portion of the cast control turned on in the event that I space out amid a specific cast and make a backfire.

Keeping in mind the end goal to figure out how to cast conventional reels without kicking back I used to hone in a field beside my residence in school. It likely looked clever yet you see a considerable measure of insane stuff going ahead at extremely inconvenient times on school grounds so individuals didn't generally give careful consideration. You truly need to invest some practice effort to get the hang of it, however once you can do it there are a great deal of favorable circumstances. Having the capacity to control the spool with your thumb permits you to make to a great degree exact throws when you get the hang of it.

In the event that you do get a kickback, don't begin pulling the distinctive circles or it will get to be difficult to get out. Begin by tenderly pulling the primary line until you locate the main circle that is halting the line. Get that circle and tenderly draw it and afterward attempt delicately pulling the fundamental line once more. Continue doing this until there are no more circles. A few people get a kick out of the chance to utilize a hook or toothpick or something sharp to choose the circles yet I generally stress over harming the line so I don't do that.

Some conventional reels (particularly bait casting reels, a subset of routine reels that fit in your grasp) have a "level wind" highlight that puts the line on the spool equally as you recover. Others don't have this component, so you need to manage the line with your fingers as you recover to abstain from having it cluster up in one territory.

My most loved bait casting reel is the Daiwa Steez. It is amazingly lightweight and extremely smooth. It is additionally extremely costly. In the more direct value extend I truly like the Daiwa Zillion arrangement. There have been numerous variants of this throughout the years; the one I have is the red 50th commemoration form. It is not as lightweight as the Steez but rather is well fabricated and smooth.

On the bigger ordinary reels, I tend to utilize Accurate reels. I like the ATD Platinum show 50 for big game trolling and draw angling. What an intense reel. On the littler end the BX 2-velocities are likewise useful for winching up huge saltwater angle. 2-speed reels permit you to move between a higher speed, bring down power recover and a lower speed, higher power recover. This can be precious when attempting to pick up line on enormous fish.

FRESHWATER FISHING LURES

If you are interested in freshwater fishing lures, you will find plenty of variety when it comes to types, colors, shapes and sizes. While most freshwater fishing lures are meant to catch bass, you can use them for other species as well. These lures can also be used to catch walleye, crappie, northern pike, muskellunge and perch. There are lures which have withstood the test of time and those that are flash in the pan successes. A box full of different lures isn't what makes a great angler; knowing what type of lure to use when does. Here are a few things to keep in mind when picking lures. Remember to consider the type of fish you want to catch and the conditions that you'll fish in.

Largemouth bass – When fishing for this type of fish, you'll need to use plastic worms. Plastic worms were invented by Nick and Cosma Crème and were first sold in 1951. Since then, they have become the most commonly used and favored lure when fishing for largemouth bass. You can buy them in all sorts of colors. They are also available in different lengths ranging from four to ten inches. In fact, thanks to plastic worms, now a plethora of other plastic lures such as crayfish, salamanders and grubs are available. While plastic worms are used most commonly in areas that have brush, timber, weeds or are located along rocky drop-offs, you can use them for surface fishing as well. You can rig them by threading the hook through the worm so that the body of the worm covers the point of the hook.

Crankbaits – You can use crankbaits in many different situations. But first you need to know what they are. Crankbaits are also known as plugs. They are artificial lures made from hard plastic. Crankbaits, as the name suggests, are meant to be cast out and then retrieved. Some types of crankbait are designed so that they can be retrieved quickly which makes fish attack them aggressively. Please note that though some types of crankbait are weed-less, they have not been designed to be used in areas that have brush, timber or weeds.

Spinnerbaits – These are designed to be used in circumstances where other bait could become tangled or hung up. Because they resemble an open safety-pin, they are also often called safety-pin spinners. Spinnerbaits normally have one or more spinners on one end and a hook and skirt on the other end which is also more weighted. You can use spinnerbaits in a variety of situations – you can pull them back quickly over the surface of the water which makes the blades splash and flash; you can bump the spinnerbait off standing timber; you can even let it fall off to the bottom when fishing from vertical structures such as drop-offs.

You can find two different types of blades when shopping for spinnerbait – teardrop-shaped blades or propeller-shaped blades. There are three types of teardrop-shaped blades. The Colorado is broad and has a rounded point at one end and is just rounded at the other. The willow-leaf has two pointed and narrow ends. The Indiana has one end that is shaped like the willow-leaf and the other end is rounded.

The French spinner or inline is a distant relation of the spinnerbait, as it were. Its body is shaped like a tube and has an Indiana or willow-leaf spinner at the front end. The back end has a skirt and treble hook. French spinners are best used in rocky areas or streams and tend to attract walleye, smallmouth bass and trout rather than largemouth bass.

Jigs – These can be used at any time of the year. Jigs have a hook that has a weighted head and usually use either a feather skirt or hair or even a plastic grub. While jigs, in general, come with rounded heads, there are jigs which are available with triangular or flat heads. These types of heads either give the jig a motion that can be described as swimming or ensure that the hook stays right side up and doesn't get caught in rocks or weeds. The most common motion used while using jigs is the up and down motion. They can be used in warm or cold water. Just remember to slow down the retrieval when fishing in colder waters. While most jigs come with a bare hook, some have a wire guard or stiff brush so that they remain weed-less. Regardless of which one you've got, the best places you can use a jig in are the ones with weeds, rocks or brush. Since they're quite cheap, losing a few jigs may not be as bad as losing say a crankbait.

Some jigs come fixed up with the safety-pin spinners that I discussed earlier. Such jigs also come equipped with a small grub body. The Bass Buster Beetle Spin is the most recognizable and common of such jigs and is quite popular not just for the eponymous bass but also for other fish species.

You can use jigs in a variety of ways for fishing. When you're fishing for bass, instead of casting long distances the way you would with other lures, flip or pitch the jig a short distance away. Retrieve the jig using a lift-and-drop movement by slowly raising and lowering the rod. Remember to keep the line taut.

You can also retrieve them straight. Keep the rod in the ten o' clock position. This gives the jig a swimming movement.

Spoons – Developed in 1850, the spoon is one of the oldest lures to be used by anglers. The story goes that it was created by someone called Julio T. Buel in New York. He made the spoon by, you guessed it, cutting the handle off a spoon and attaching a hook to the bowl. The motion of the spoon is a side to side wobble during retrieval; this motion attracts the fish to it. Since they come in different sizes, you can use the larger spoons to fish for large fish such as pike, bass and walleye and the smaller ones for fish such as panfish and trout.

Flies – Flies are best used when going after trout. A fly has one hook which comes with a skirt or a feather. Flies are the lightest and smallest types of lure available. They are used mostly when fishing in streams for trout. A special rod is used and the fly is attached to a weighted line along with a monofilament leader. Since trout feed on many different species of flies, artificial flies are available in many different patterns as well. Experienced anglers often make their own flies, sometimes right on the spot so that they can 'match the hatch'. There are five different types of flies – dry flies, wet flies, nymphs, streamers and bugs.

You don't have to stick to one type of fly; you can use two or three different types to see what type of fly the fish are biting. You can try different combinations but be sure to check the local regulations about how many lures you are allowed to have on your line at one time.

When choosing your lure, there are a couple of things you'll need to keep in mind.

First of all, keep in mind the type of water conditions and weather you will be encountering. When determining what colors to buy, keep this adage in mind, "light day, light colors, dark day, dark colors". If you're going to be spending a bright and sunny day fishing and the water is clear, buy lures that are patterned upon nature and are lighter colored. However, if a cloudy day is your day of choice and the water is murky, choose colors that are darker and non-natural. Also try to choose lures that vibrate or make some noise.

There is an exception to this rule. You can use two-toned plastic worms when fishing in murky water. Such worms have a dark head color and a fluorescent yellow or pink tail color.

Secondly, keep in mind the tackle you plan to use and the species you plan to fish for. A good rule of thumb is to use crankbaits and spinnerbaits when going after bigger fish such as pike and bass and smaller grubs and jigs when fishing for panfish such as perch, crappie and bluegill. If you're using ultralight or light spin casting or spinning tackle or fly rods (dry and wet flies) with four to ten-pound test lines, it's a good idea to use smaller lures. On the other hand, if you're using medium or heavy action rods, bait casting or spinning reels and ten to twelve-pound test lines, you'll need the larger lures.

The size of the lure is often determined by how fish react to weather conditions. In times such as early spring or cold front conditions when the skies are clear and the waters are colder, the fish are lethargic. In such times, it's better to use smaller lures rather than the larger ones. If you're planning to go ice-fishing, you'll need really tiny lures such as small spoons or grub jigs. If you're experiencing high-winds, you might want to go with a larger lure. This ensures that there is enough resistance at the end of the line so that the wind doesn't bow it, making it impossible for you to determine whether fish are hitting the lure. You can also try casting out a spinner and then just casting and retrieving the lure.

CHAPTER 5

FISHING RIGS

A rig is the name given to an arrangement of the items that are utilized for angling. It is generally made up of at least one line, hook, sinker, bobber, swivel, lure, beads and other such tackle used for fishing. A rig may be held by a rod, by hand, or even attached to a pontoon or dock. A few rigs are intended to coast close to the surface of the water, others are intended to sink to the very bottom. A few rigs are intended for trolling. Numerous rigs are outlined particularly to catch a specific type of fish, yet will function admirably for a wide range of other species as well.

Despite all the advancements made in the fishing scene, now and again only a plain ol' hook, weight and bobber with a hunk of worm, minnow or bloodsucker will get more fish. One of the greatest mix-ups made by the novice fisher is over rigging, utilizing too expansive of a hook, heavier than required weight with an unnecessarily large bobber showing an unnatural look, decreases the capacity to distinguish angle strikes in their angling presentation. The best application is to choose the lightest conceivable terminal handle appropriate for the condition and the types of fish.

BOBBERS (FLOATS)

Angling with a bobber is one the most well-known and basic set-ups. The depth is set beforehand and the bobber or float presents the bait at that depth. It also acts as an indicator when a fish bites. You can find a variety of shapes, colors and sizes in bobbers today. There are glow or lighted bobber if you want to go fishing at night, slip bobbers that the angling line goes through for deep water angling and the fixed bobber that uses snap or spring lock for shallow water fishing.

SLIDER SINKER RIG

This is maybe the most famous base rig utilized anyplace as a part of the world because of it's straightforward development and adequacy. Most tie their rig utilizing a blend of hook, leader, empty sinker and barrel swivel. By and by, I am not for excessively numerous terminal handles on a rig. Wanting to have quite recently the insignificant, I tie mine contrastingly as I'll delineate here.

The purpose behind the rig's adequacy is it will permit the fish to draw bait delicately without spooking it. Along these lines, the fisherman will know whether there is a take and inspire prepared to set the hook. With a hover hook, there is no compelling reason to set the hook as the circle-hooks are composed in such a way fish will hook themselves on the lips when they attempt to spit the bait out.

Under what conditions would it be a good idea for me to utilize a Sliding Sinker Rig?

* when the fundamental base rig is too light and you have to cast to a further separation.

* when you have to introduce a littler, lighter bait so you require a sinker on your rig.

* in waterways or saltwater angling.

The segments to amass the rig

Size# 1/0 circle hook. (Conform measure as indicated by target angle.)

15" of 50lb clear mono leader of width 0.65mm.

28" of 20lb clear mono line of width 0.30mm

Long oval empty sinker. (Alter estimate as indicated by throwing separation and bait measure)

STEP1

Snell the hook with the 50lb mono leader. With a 0.65mm measurement leader, you can be guaranteed of getting even some toothy fishes any semblance of Pacu and Snakeheads which will require them some push to gnaw off. It would likewise be less obvious contrasted with follow wires.

STEP2

Join the 50lb leader with the 20lb line utilizing an Albright tie. Make around 20 swings to frame the Albright. For more grounded and more secured join, apply some quick 4min dry paste onto the bunch. [Optional] You might need to include a globule top of the Albright. Guidelines on the most proficient method to tie an Albright Knot

STEP3

Embed 20lb line through the sinker and slide it down to the Albright hitch zone. The much thicker breadth of the Albright bunch will hold the sinker set up without it sliding the distance down to the hook. In the event that the sinker's emptied gap is still bigger than the Albright tie, simply utilize a couple of pincers to pleat and fix the opening to decrease the breadth only a smidgen yet the sinker is still ready to slide up and down with insignificant contact.

Done! You are prepared to fish.

3-WAY RIG

The three way rig is a standout amongst the most surely understood catfish rigs. In the event that you make a few inquiries you'll see that numerous individuals believe it's the best way to rig yet that couldn't possibly be more off-base.

Fame of the three way rig has a considerable measure to do with deception go around among fishermen. It additionally doesn't help that handle shops push pre-tied three path rigs in ranges where they're offering fabricated catfish baits and other catfishing tackle and rigging.

The customary three way rig requires the utilization of three way swivels. It can be tedious to tie as a result of the measure of bunches included yet "conventional" three way rigs utilize three way swivels.

Notwithstanding the conventional three path rig there's numerous varieties of this rig dispense with the utilization of the 3-way swivel.

The three way rig will get angle yet it's regularly utilized more than it ought to be, particularly the customary rig.

More experienced catfish fishers regularly depend on other catfish rigs or more propelled varieties of the three way rig. In case you're just going to learn or depend on one catfish rig then there's a vastly improved alternative that is the crucial "go to" catfish rig.

Underneath you'll discover more subtle elements on rigging the three way rig utilizing both a customary and altered form.

Simply ensure you invest some energy adapting a portion of the other catfish rigs as you'll likely observe them to be more powerful getting catfish by and large.

When To Use The Three Way Rig

The three way rig is intended for circumstances where you have to keep your bait off of the base.

It can be utilized for tied down angling or float angling and will work for every one of the three types of catfish in lakes, stores and waterways.

Handle Needed

Here's an essential rundown of terminal handle required.

Leader Line – Like Offshore Angler Tight Line – 1/2 lb. Spools in 40 Lb Test

Barrel Swivel

Three-Way Brass Swivel

Favored Hook

Weight (Sinker)

Monofilament leader line

Step by step instructions to Tie The Three Way Rig

To tie this rig you have to first cut your leader line that will keep running from the base of the swivel to the weight (sinker).

Your line running from the base of it should be longer than the leader that will keep running from your hook to your swivel.

For this illustration we are going to cut the line from the swivel to the weight at eighteen inches. Connect the weight line to the base of the three route swivel toward one side and afterward append the sinker on the flip side.

Presently cut your leader line for your hook. For this reason we are going to utilize a twelve crawl line. Append the leader line to the side of the three way swivel and after that join the hook to the inverse end of this line.

Attach your mainline to the highest point of the three way swivel.

There's an assortment of bunches you can utilize. You can take in every one of the points of interest on the best bunches to use here.

Other Three Way Rig Options

A few fishers utilize a light weight line from racing to the sinker. This is done as such if the weight catches, the line can be broken effortlessly relinquishing the weight however sparing whatever remains of the catfish rig.

You can include a 2" split froth peg float to the leader line a couple inches from the hook to help with bait presentation too. This is a typical handle thing utilized as a part of numerous catfish rigs like the Santee Rig.

In case you're floating looking for catfish utilizing this setup then another option is to utilize a snag-less float angling sinker rather than other customary sinker sorts. The snag-less float angling sinkers will as a rule help to extraordinarily diminish the quantity of obstacles you experience when floating.

TROLLING RIGS

For some fishermen and contract commanders trolling has dependably been one the best angling strategies by showing at least one lures to quantities of diversion fish at an exact profundity or spread out over a huge territory. There are two key basics for a decent discover, trolling at the correct speed, and profundity of the proper lure decision. With the cutting edge advancements of trolling rigging and handle today fishermen no longer need to think about how profound or how quick their lure is running.

TROLLING TOOLS

Downriggers

Downriggers are used especially to ensure that the trolling depth is consistent. A downrigger is an arrangement of a mechanism that is winch-like. A cable is fed off a rolling reel.

The feed goes through a guide system that is laid the length of an extension arm. At the end of the cable, you'll find an attached weight. The weight has the line release attached to it. You attach a fishing line from a separate reel and rod to the release system which is located on the downrigger cable. To drop the line to the depth you want, you need to lower the weight. There is a footage counter that is coupled with the reel unit. It tells you exactly how much cable you have released. Once you hit the depth you want, it locks the reel in place.

Trolling Boards

When a boat moves over fish, they respond by swimming to one or the other side. Trollers have two choices to increase the reach of the trolling pattern. There are trolling boards that plane to one side on a separate cord. Something called planer mast holds the cord onboard. You then need to attach a fishing line or lines to the cord. You can do this by means of manufactured line releases or rubber bands and wire loops. When the boat moves forward, the release slides down to where you want it. When a fish bites, the release is tripped so that the fish can be fought on a line that is free.

ONLINE SIDE PLANERS

A line release (tension clip/clip on) is used to attach onside planers to the fishing line. The planers level to the side when the boat moves forward. When a fish bites, the board is released, and it moves down the line. It then hits a bead or swivel that is quite a distance from the lure.

Both side planers and trolling boards ensure that you can run more than one line from the aft of the boat, thus covering a larger area.

JUMPING PLANES

Also known as a Dipsey Diver, a jumping plane is a diving device that is circular in shape. It tracks straight, left or right, depending upon how the rudder is set. You need to tie the line directly to the front eye of the plane and then snap on a release. You need to use a leader to attach the lure to the rear eye. When a fish bites, the front eye is released which, in turn, flattens the diving plane. You can then reel in the fish without having to pull against the dive setting of the plane.

FISHING WEIGHTS AND LINES

Lead Core (Weighted Trolling Line)

The lead core first was first used in fishing during the 1970s as a weighted trolling line. It meant that fishing enthusiasts who were fishing for lake trout, walleye, steelhead and salmon to use shallow running, light weight baits such as balsa, spoons, and plastic minnow lures could reach the depths where these fish could be found. A lead core has two components. There is the inner wire that is made of pliable and soft lead. Then there is the outer sheath that is made of nylon braid. The nylon braid is color coded for metering purposes every ten yards. These color codes are known as term colors. Since lead can be harmful to the environment, a non-lead, environmentally safe line has recently been introduced. It has a metal alloy instead of lead. You can get weighted trolling lines in spools that range from a hundred to two hundred yards and range from twelve-pound to forty-five pound test ratings.

How much weighted trolling line you need depends entirely on what fish you want to go after and what depth you want to target. For instance, if you want to fish for Great Lakes walleye you can use thirty yards of weighted line or about three colors. If, on the other hand, you're going after salmon you may need the entire two hundred yards or twenty colors. A good rule of thumb to follow based on the pound test is that every two yards of the weighted line will sink one foot. The conventional level wind trolling reel is the only type of reel that you can use for the weighted trolling line. The species of fish you target will determine the line capacity (bigger for salmon, smaller for walleye). A line backing must be used whenever you're spooling the reel. This ensures that the reel is filled with the proper amount of line. The super braid is the most popular line backing in use today. An Albright knot is used to tie it to the weighted line. A fluorocarbon or monofilament leader is tied using a Uni knot once the weighted line has been spooled. The entire setup is called "segmented." When this is placed properly, it positions the weighted line and the lure to the correct depth where the fish feed.

Trolling weighted line involves a precision and technique that requires both knowledge and skill. If you want to utilize the trolling technique, it might be a good idea to research the area you plan to fish in and the species you want to go for before you buy your gear.

WIRE FISHING LINE

A trolling line option that you can consider if you're planning to fish in deep waters is wire. There are two types of wireline: stranded and solid. Solid wire is also known as Monel. A nickel-copper alloy, it can go to depths that are more than stranded wire depending upon the ultra thin line weight and diameter. Stranded wire is made of copper or stainless steel. It comes in forty-nine strands and three and seven strands. Sometimes it is coated with vinyl and is used mainly as leader material. The seven stranded six braided wire is one of the most well-liked wire lines when it comes to freshwater fishing. If you don't want to use lead core and are looking for an alternative, you can consider the copper seven strand. Since the weight of the copper wire is twice that of the lead core, you need half the amount of line to get to the same depth. Wireline has many advantages over usual lines such as monofilament or braided. First of all, a wireline uses less line. Its ultra thin diameter and the heavy weight of copper combine to allow it to cut through water easily and go deeper. Secondly, the line stretch is low, so you know exactly when a fish bites.

A wire line requires specialized equipment. Reels need to have a stainless steel or metal spool that can hold the wire line. They also need to be trolling level wind. Rods need to have either line guides that use rollers or hardened line guides so that the wire won't cut them. If you're planning to use wire in your trolling rig, I recommend that you visit a professional shop that deals specifically in wire line rods and reels.

One of the most frequent problems faced by a lot of people who use wire is spooling the wire and backing on the reel properly. However, if you go fishing with sufficient information and the proper rig, the wire will be an asset to you and help you increase the rate of your catch.

SNAP ON WEIGHTS

When you're flat line trolling, and you want to ensure your bait gets to where the salmon, bass, trout, muskies, and walleyes are suspended you should use snap weights. Snap weights or snap-on weights are a removable weight system. The weights are on the heavier side, ranging from half to eight pounds. They snap onto the line using a spring tension clamp, and hence the name. When a fish bites, you retrieve the line to the snap weight, which is then unclipped from the line so that you can fight the fish. Since a variety of weights are available, you have access to an array of depth settings without having to re-rig your rod. You can start with the fifty-fifty approach wherein you place the snap weight halfway on the line. When the weight is moved closer to the lure, the lure responds that much more to the motion of the boat and that of your rod. When the weight is further away from the lure, it is less responsive to the boat and more responsive to the actions of the waves and the wind. The further away the snap weight is from the lure, the less chance there is of the fish getting scared of biting. You can use snap weights on lead lines, braided lines, and fluorocarbon/monofilament.

INLINE TROLLING WEIGHT

Inline trolling weights or sinkers are another choice when you want to troll at a particular depth. These incorporate a down weighted keel design that stabilizes the weight when it moves in the water and prevents it from wobbling unnecessarily. The good quality trolling sinkers come equipped with bead type swivels and chains that make sure that there is minimal line twist and don't allow the action of the lure to be inhibited, which can happen if the majority of the weight hangs below the line.

TEXAS RIG

Not only does the Texas rig give the worm a straight profile, but it is also popular because of the fact that it has weed-less properties. A Texas rig is supposed to be weighted, although it is used by many anglers without a weight. These anglers do rig their worm "Texas style" by utilizing the weed-less feature of the rig.

If you don't want to or plan to use a weight, then you just need a hook to rig a worm in the Texas style. Later, we'll discuss the advantages and disadvantages of using a weight but let's focus on how to rig the hook right now.

Best Hooks For Texas Rigging

Although a straight shank hook can be used to Texas rig a worm, your best bet to keep the head of the worm from sliding down the shank is the offset hook. Offset hooks come in two types — wide gap hooks and round bend hooks. Wide gap hooks show more hook to the fish while round bend hooks show less hook.

When rigging Texas style, the angles will differ depending upon which of the two types of hooks you're using. If you're using a wide gap hook, you'll want to enter straight in but with a round bend hook you'll need to enter at a forty-five-degree angle. You can use a 3/0 hook for most worms.

Best Weights For Texas Rigging

The depth that you want and the rate at which the worm sinks are determined by the weight. For most rigs in general, and for the Texas rig, in particular, you'll need to use bullet weights. These weights slide on the line before the hook is tied and they sit at the head of the worm.

You can use the bullet weight in three ways – let it slide freely on the line itself, peg it at a certain distance away from the worm and peg it to the nose of the worm. Depending upon how you want the worm to be presented at the bottom, you can decide how to set the weight.

While pegging the weight to the nose of the worm will put it right on the bottom, you might want to stop and consider the fact that sometimes keeping the worm suspended off the bottom is more advantageous. Let's take an example. Say there is grass on the bottom that is eight inches tall. In such a case, it might be a good idea to set the weight about ten inches from the worm. This will ensure that the worm doesn't disappear in the grass when the weight hits bottom. Instead, the worm will sink naturally and slowly to the tips of the grass.

Step by step instructions to Texas Rig A Worm

To demonstrate this, I am using a wide gap hook. In order to rig the worm, you'll need to insert the tip of the hook straight through the nose of the worm and go in about a quarter of an inch. Now, while this penetration isn't bad, the ideal penetration is when the distance from the eyelet of the hook to where the hook bends is matched.

After the penetration, turn the point of the hook ninety degrees and make it come out of the side of the worm. Remember that the side you choose for the exit has to be opposite to the side that the hook point will be exposed on once the rig is ready. If you're using a basic worm which has a round body, the side doesn't matter. However, if you want the hook to be exposed on a specific side and the worm isn't rounded you'll need to keep this point in mind.

Once the tip of the hook is out, you need to slide the head of the worm up the shank. Once the head reaches the eyelet of the hook, stop. This is where things become absolutely critical. If you want to keep the worm looking natural and straight, it must be entered at the right location. Here's how you do it.

Let the worm hang in line with the hook's bottom end. Make sure that it is hanging freely. Hold the hook upright from the middle of the shank. Whichever part of the bottom of the hook lines up with the body of the worm is the distance that you need to enter the worm. The distance must be calculated from the head of the worm. Hold the worm between your finger and thumb. Position your thumb at the point that marks the distance from the head so that you know where to enter from.

Don't let the worm twist as you enter. This isn't a problem with most plastic worms since they have a straight line running from the head to the tail which you can use as a reference to make sure that the worm is, in fact, straight.

Once you know where you want the hook tip to penetrate the worm for the second time, you just need to push the point of the hook straight into the body of the worm. When the point comes out, you'll need to straighten the worm. This ensures that the body of the worm and the tip of the hook set in a straight line with each other.

At this point the rig is ready. However, if you want to make it more weed-less, a good way to do it is to bury the tip of the hook just under the plastic.

CAROLINA RIGS

This rig is probably the most well-liked rig when it comes to fishing for bass regardless of whether you're an amateur or a professional. Amateurs may find the rig a bit too complex for recreational purposes, however, and so many of them choose simpler and easier rigs. Contrary to this perception though, the Carolina rig is not complex at all, and it has advantages that a fisherman of any proficiency would be sorry to miss. The reason the Carolina rig has gained the reputation of being "complicated" is that there is such endless debate and analysis that it can be quite overwhelming. Don't be misled. The rig is versatile in its uses, and if you don't have it, you are missing a powerful asset indeed. In actual fact, the Carolina rig is a simple and easy rig that has a lot of advantages. Let's see if this can't be made easy for you.

The first thing we have to do is get down to basics and figure out what it's made of. Once you know the components, all you have to comprehend is the role that each component plays in the rig. Then it becomes really easy. So let's start.

Off-Set Worm Hook – You don't need to start looking into exactly what bait and what hook size you should have. Just make sure that the size of the hook works with the size of the bait you're planning to use. If you want specifics, you can go online to find out the exact information. I recommend that you follow that age old advice – use common sense. Don't complicate matters.

Bait – The first thing to remember here is that you should use only plastic bait that is soft. You can decide exactly which one you want. If something has worked well for you in the past, pick that. Here's a tip. Determine the bait based on water conditions – lighter colors for water that is quite clear and darker colors for muddy water.

Leader – The leader for a Carolina rig needs to be anywhere between twelve to forty-eight inches. The line between the swivel and the hook is known as the leader. The most important part here is that you can't choose the length of the leader at random. Whatever the length of the leader, your bait will float the same length above the bottom. For example, say the fish are around twelve inches from the bottom. Your leader will also need to be twelve inches. This ensures that the bait floats right in front of their faces. You can use a fish finder to get that information, but if you don't have one, then eighteen inches is a good length. You also need to make sure that the fish can't see the leader and that it doesn't break if it goes over rough terrain. It is best to get one that is at least seventeen pounds and that has low stretch.

Swivel – The whole point of a swivel is that the line shouldn't twist. On the Carolina rig, however, it serves another purpose. Here it is meant as a stop to the weight. Therefore, invisibility to the bass becomes a critical factor when you go to buy a swivel. Black colored swivels are the best for this purpose. Of course, size also matters. The bigger it is, the more chances that the bass will see it. But at the same time, you don't want to get one that is too small to do its job. However, don't fret over it too much. If you don't have a black swivel, use what you have. Remember, don't complicate matters.

Glass Bead – This is another one of the don't-fret-if-you-don't-have-it components. Overall, it's not essential to the working of the Carolina rig. A glass bead is there for two reasons – a) so that it can collide with the weight to send a signal out to the bass that dinner is here, and b) so that the knot isn't damaged by the weight. If you're fishing in clear water and stealth is important, leave out the bead. If you're fishing in murky waters, keep it so that the bass know where to come to bite.

Weight or Bullet Sinker – Well, the purpose of the bait is sort-of implied in its name. It is what sends your line towards the bottom and keeps it there until you decide to move it around. The weight is important to the rig. I recommend that you use a 3/8 to a one-ounce bullet head tungsten sinker. Use a lighter weight in shallower waters and a heavier weight in deeper ones. If you're confused, just go for a three-fourth pound weight. It should be enough. What you need to remember about the weight is this – you are connected to the bottom of the water body that you're fishing in through the pole in your hands. You have to be able to feel it – kind of like a blind person senses the obstacles at the end of their cane. The reason I recommend the tungsten sinker is that it helps you get this feel.

These are all the components you will find in a Carolina rig. Each one has been the subject of endless debate. If you don't want to get confused by what different people are saying, I would recommend that you follow what I've stated above. Don't get drawn into the endless arguments that swirl around the uses, advantages and disadvantages of each component. Don't complicate matters.

Strategy

Now that you know the components let's take a look at the technique. If you want to be successful with this rig, the bait needs to move almost at a snail's pace. This part is critical. You can't use the retrieval of the reel to achieve this snail's pace. The whole key is how you move the pole. Essentially, the weight needs to be dragged along the bottom extremely slowly. Move the pole either to the left or to the right and then forward, very slightly. Remember to keep the line tight while doing this. You can vary this movement by giving the pole a quick jerk at decent intervals. This makes the bait move very fast and can trigger the bass into attacking it. If you think you have a bite, you need to ensure that the slack is reeled in as fast as possible and then move your pole in a side sweep so that the hook is set. Again, remember to keep the line tight while doing this. The next time you cast the distance should be the same as the length of the leader from the last point you cast to.

Benefits of the Carolina Rig

Frankly, I believe that this is the best rig to use to keep the bait on the bottom. Secondly, the changes in the length of the leader ensure that the bait is presented right in front of the bass. The best part is that using this method ensures that you cover a large area. As such, you'll find many veterans of this sport using the rig as a means of "finding." First, locate the bass using this rig. Then switch to whatever bait will work best in that situation. Of course, the rig cannot conjure up bass. If they aren't on the bottom, the rig won't work.

Now you're basically prepared to angle, yet in the event that you need to make the rig more weed-less you can bury the tip of the hook only somewhat under the surface of the plastic.

CONCLUSION

And here we are, at the end. This is by no means all that you can learn about fishing. You could spend your entire life just fishing and still not learn all the secrets that the waters of this world have. That doesn't mean that you can't try though and have fun while doing it.

I hope you've enjoyed reading this book as much as I've enjoyed writing it. Do leave a review to let me know what you think.

FREE BONUS: "Click The Link Below To Receive Your Bonus

https://publishfs.leadpages.co/pangea-health/

Made in the USA
San Bernardino, CA
05 February 2017